Journal belongs to:

Date:

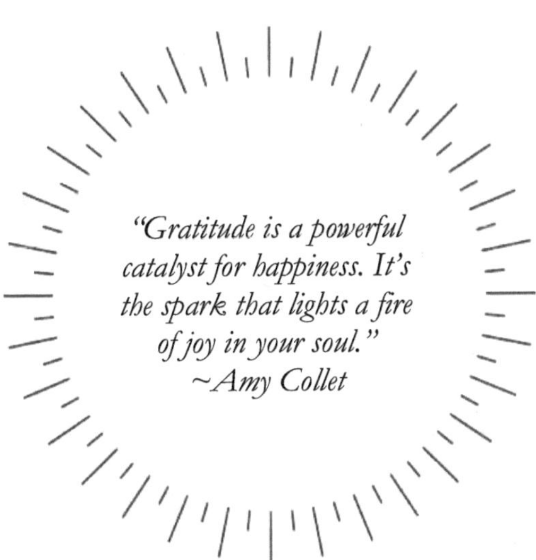

Unlock the magic of your gratitude journal. This is a space to write your thoughts, dreams, inspirations, daily observations, travels, opinions, and everything you're grateful for. This practice helps you grow and reflect on how far you've come on your life's journey.

As you journal, you might begin to see your daily activities in a new light. You may start noticing the little things that bring you happiness, like a simple sunset.

May you cultivate joy, peace, and love as you unveil your most authentic self. Embracing gratitude is a small but powerful step toward a life of true fulfillment. By focusing on what you're thankful for, you invite more prosperity into your life. Enjoy the ride!

Grateful for new beginnings: Date:

Date:

Date:

Date:

Date:

Date:

Date:

Date:

Date:

Date:

Date:

Date:

Date:

Date:

Date:

Date:

Date:

Date:

Date:

Date:

Date:

Date:

Date:

Date:

Date:

Date:

Date:

Date:

Date:

Date:

Date:

Date:

Date:

Date:

Date:

Date:

Date:

Date:

Date:

Date:

Date:

Date:

Date:

Date:

Date:

Date:

Date:

Date:

Date:

Date:

Date:

Date:

Check the first page to see your progress! Date:

ISBN: 978-1-7361005-1-6 (Paperback)
Library of Congress upon request
Book & cover design by Indie Publishing, LLC
Editing by Ann Winfrey

Printed by Amazon in the United States of America
First printed edition 2024
Indie Publishing, LLC